T0042363

Making Tortillas

Michelle Freeman

Jordan and I are going to make tortillas.
We need all of these things.

spoon

bowl

salt

oil

baking powder

spatula

skillet

paper towel

warm water

flour

rolling pin

First, Jordan puts the flour, salt, and baking powder in a bowl.
I stir them together.
Then, we add the oil and water.
We stir it to make a dough.

I press and roll the dough.
This makes the dough smooth and stretchy
Then, we shape the dough into balls.

I flatten the balls with a rolling pin. Tortillas are round and flat.

Mom cooks the tortillas.
Then, she puts them on a paper towel
to drain.

We all helped make the tortillas.
We all help eat the tortillas, too.